Your Hands, My Hell

Possession, Obsession, Damnation

Khirawadhi

BookLeaf Publishing
India | USA | UK

Made with ❤ on the BookLeaf Publishing Platform
www.bookleafpub.in
www.bookleafpub.com

Dedication

To the ones who ache in silence,
who tremble beneath hands that both heal and hurt.

To the ones who kneel—not in weakness, but in worship.
To those who crave love with claws,
who taste devotion in bruises,
and know that surrender is the most erotic kind of power.

This is for the soft who begged to be ruined.
For the ruined who found softness in the wreckage.
For the lovers who never needed safe—only real.

These pages are stained with your ache.
May you find yourself undone within them.
And may you call that undoing divine.

— Khirawadhi

Preface

Love is not always gentle.
It doesn't always soothe.
Sometimes it bruises. Sometimes it binds. Sometimes it breaks—
and still, we ache for it.

This collection is for those who know that passion cuts both ways.
That devotion can become a cage. That pleasure often carries the taste of pain.

These poems were born in the shadows—
where obsession tightens like a noose,
where worship leaves scars,
and where lovers consume each other whole.

I wrote these pages without armor.
Every poem is a wound, a hunger, a truth I never hid.

This is my vulnerability—and I'm not afraid of it.
Not anymore.

If you've ever loved recklessly—
if you've ever craved what could ruin you—

then these pages were always yours.

Welcome to the hunger.

To deepen the descent, let these songs bleed into the silence:

"One of the Girls" – The Weeknd
"Shameless" – Camila Cabello
"Crazy in Love" (Cover) – Sofia Karlberg
"You Want Me" - XV Nauthiz

Acknowledgements

This book was born of fire—
the fire of desire, the ache of longing,
the exquisite pain of a love that refuses to die.
To the ghosts of my past,
and the obsessions that still linger—
thank you for carving your names into my soul.
You were my torment and my muse.

To the readers—
you who crave love in its rawest, most dangerous form—
this is for you.
For those who've tasted devotion laced with suffering,
who've chased passion even as it scorched—
I see you. I write for you.

To those who stood beside me
when my words bled too dark, too deep—
your faith kept me from drowning.

You know who you are.

And to love itself—reckless, cruel, intoxicating—
thank you for giving me both ruin and rapture.

I would not trade the wreckage for anything less real.

1. Heat Between Floors

He looks at me with a hunger
already undressed me in his mind.
His gaze, lingers—
slow, dark, deliberate—
dragging over my skin
until I shiver beneath it.

The elevator hums,
but all I feel is tension—
thick, pulsing, undeniable.
He steps closer.
I don't step back.
His breath brushes mine,
and my body answers
before he even touches me.

My back hits the mirrored wall—
his hand sliding beneath my skirt,
knuckles grazing bare skin,
palm pressing heat

into my stomach.
Then he kisses me—
slow at first, like he's savoring the ruin,
then deeper, filthier.
I melt. Dizzy. Knees weak
as his fingers
find their way home.

2. Say When

I won't resist tonight—
the lock clicks behind us,
and already,
my knees
forget how to stand.

Touch me like I'm breakable,
then break me slowly—
with fingers
that whisper before they claim.

I've undressed more than skin for you—
I've laid down my need,
soft,
trembling,
begging to be taken.
Your breath brushes my neck,
and I lean—
offering, aching— a quiet
"yes"

in the way my body tilts.

Let me feel the gravity of
your want,
the storm right before surrender.
Say when—
and I'll fall apart in
your hands.

3. Taken, Gently

Your hands
find my hips
like they've known them forever—
sure,
grounding,
claiming.

I arch
—not to escape,
but to feel every inch of you
pressed into the ache
I've carried all day.

You part my thighs like pages
—not to read,
but to write your name between them.

Your mouth lowers
—warm,
reverent—

lips like a prayer,
tongue like confession.

I gasp,
caught betweenbeing touched
and being understood.

And when your tongue claims me,
I forget how to speak
—but remember how to feel.

4. Ruined Softly

You hold me still—
not rough, but firm,
like you're afraid
I'll disappear
if you blink.

Your hand finds home
between my thighs,
but your eyes—
they never leave mine.

Every gasp I give,
you drink slow,
like it's sacred.
You whisper,
"Let go."
And I do—
shaking,
moaning,
as your lips part me open

where only trust dares to go

5. Afterglow

You collapse beside me,
still catching your breath—
your hand,
trembling,
never leaving my skin.

My thighs still ache
where your name echoed,
where your mouth
beggedinstead of spoke.

I turn to you—
bare,
wrecked,
but glowing.

You touch my face
like you can't believe
you just owned it.

And when you kiss me,
it's not hunger–
it's reverence.
You don't say
"mine."
You don't have to.
I already am.

6. Worship in Ruin

You light a cigarette
with fingers that still shake,
watching me
from the foot of the bed
like I'm something
sacred—
or something damned.

I'm still open.
Still wet from you.
Legs parted in the sheets
like an offering you forgot to close.
You crawl back up,
eyes glazed,
lips parted,
not to kiss—
but to kneel.
"Again,"
you rasp.
Not a request.

A prayer.

And when your mouth finds me,
slow and starving,
I arch—
not from pleasure,
but surrender.
Because this?
This isn't fucking anymore.

This is devotion
drenched in sweat,
and I am your altar—
rebuilt in every moan.

7. I Devour You

I crawl into your lap
like temptation
dressed in skin,
my mouth
already parted—
hungry,
slow,
sinful.

Your breath catches
when I lick the tip—
not to tease,
but to taste powerfrom its source.
I take you in—
inch by aching inch—
tongue worshipping,
lips sealed tight
like I'm claiming you
with every wet pull.

Your head falls back,
fingers buried in my hair—
helpless,
undone,
as I feast like a woman
starved for your ruin.

And when you try to warn me,
your voice breaking—
I just hum around you,
eyes locked,
saying without a word:
"I'm not done until you beg."

8. The Undoing of Him

Your chest still heaves,
but now
it's my hand
guiding your breath back to steady.

You're trembling—
not from what I did to you,
but from how fullyyou let it happen.

I trace the sweat at your temple,
kiss your jaw like it's glass,
and whisper nothing—
because words would shatter you more.

You try to hide it—
the way your eyes gloss over,
the way surrender lingerslong after release.
So I hold you.

Not soft, not strong—

just right.
Just enough.
Until your heartbeatfinds
its way backinside my palm.

9. Choke on Desire (Visual Recall)

I lie back—
legs parted, breath shallow—
two fingers on my throat,
where your grip still bruises me in memory.
Your voice echoes—low, cruel, perfect.

"Look at you... loving this."

My lips part.
I do.
I hate how much.
My other hand slides lower—
slow at first, just like you did—
teasing,
threatening,
until my hips lift off the bed on their own.
I squeeze my neck—
not tight,
just enough to feel

how empty the air gets without you.
And in that blur of lightheaded want,
I slide my fingers in—
wet, aching,
yours in my mind.

I arch. I moan.
I forget I'm alone.
And when I finally scream,
I bite my wrist
to stop the sound—
just like you made me.

10. Starving Without Her

He strokes himself in the dark,
jaw clenched,
breath uneven,
her name trapped somewhere between his teeth.

Fingers grip tighter—
but it's not her hand,
not her mouth,
not enough.
He pictures her—
sprawled,
ruined,
gasping beneath him,
the way she moaned
when he owned her throat.

His hips jerk,
a curse escapes,
but it dies in his mouth
like she did in his bed—

delirious, shaking, undone.

Release crashes—
brief, brutal—
but he stays hard.
Still aching.
Still hers.

11. Rain Between Our Bodies

Nights blur—
your name, my fingers,
your moans imagined behind closed eyes.
You fuck your fist. I ride my hand.
But it's not us.
Not this.
Not enough.

You whisper my name into your palm,
while I moan yours into the shower wall—
steam rising, thighs trembling,
soaking more than skin.

Every red light, I close my eyes.
You in my lap. Me in your mouth.
We touch ourselves in traffic,
clutching memories that make us ruin.

Then one night—

no warnings, no words—
just rain.
You find me.
I run to you.
And we fuck like it's war.
Like we'll die tomorrow.

Tongues tangled, drenched clothes pulled apart,
you lift me against a brick wall
and slam every second we missed
back inside me.
We don't say ***"I missed you."***
We say it with every thrust,
every gasp,
every scream the rain tries to swallow.

12. Velvet Sin Beneath the Linen

Candlelight dances on our wine,
but it's her hand beneath the linen
that robs me of breath—
knuckles grazing fire
no one else is allowed to witness.
soft, lethal—
a mouth painted in promisesunder the table.

I speak in fragments,
my voice pulled taut—
fork untouched,
while she dineson the ache beneath my belt.
Each touch is deliberate,
press, pause, stroke—
and I can't decideif I want to beg or break.

My hands grip the edge of the table.
Jaw clenched.Pulse a war drum
under starched linen and civility.

The waiter asks if I'd like dessert.
She answers for me—
crossing her legs with a smilesharp as a blade.
My name—dies in my throat.
My control—splinters between her fingers.
I lean in, unraveling:
"Stop."
She tilts her head and whispers,
"Not until you surrender."
check arrives—
my breath is ragged,
my world undone.
She licks her fingertip,
brushes it across her lower lip,
and purrs,
"Darling, you were always the main course."

13. Backseat Benediction

Rain taps the roof—
soft, steady—
but inside, it's chaos.
My fingers slide back in—
two, then three—
and you gasp, arch,
leaking all over the leather
filthy and holy beneath my hands.

You ride them,
desperate—
moaning against my neck,
biting my collarlike it'll save you.
And I'm soaked too—
throbbing, pulsing,
pants barely unzipped,
grinding into your thigh
like I'll lose my mind if I don't get in you now.

"I can't—fuck,

I'm gonna—"
you choke out, trembling.
I clamp a hand over your mouth,
smirk darkly against your ear.

"Not yet. Not until I do."

And I thrust—deep, full, brutal—
making you scream into my palm
as you tighten, soaking me in a rush.

The windows fog.
The world disappears.
You fall against me—wrecked, wet, divine.
And I whisper like a final command:

"Now you're mine.All over again."

14. Aftertaste

I push you against the door—
mouth at your throat,
hand back between your thighs,
claiming what's mine again
before you can beg.

You gasp.
You plead.
You leak against my palm
like you were made for this.
By the time I press you into the sheets,
you're already gone—
moaning,
twitching,
begging for mercy
you know I'll never give.

"Open wider,"

I growl into your ear,

"and show me where heaven dies."

15. The First Sip of Sin

your name still burns my mouth
like the first sip of sin.
too sweet, too strong—
and still, i swallow.

I used to pray for release.
now i beg to be kept—
right here.
beneath you,
inside your shadow,
between the ache and the answer.
You kissed me
like a man digging his own grave—
slow, grateful, greedy.
and god, i let you.

You made pain feel like poetry,
made ruin feel like ritual.
your hands didn't just touch—
they testified.

each bruise a sermon,
each breath a vow,
and when i asked what we were,
you said:

"this is the part where heaven dies."

so i stayed.
burned.
loved you like a hymn turned into hunger,
and i still do.
quietly. violently. eternally.
your name tastes like sin
and i keep it on my tongue—
dripping, throbbing, holy.

16. Stolen Moments Behind the Garden Wall

We weren't supposed to be here.
Private property. Gated estate.
But you pulled me through the break in the wall—
grinning like sin wrapped in sunlight.
You wasted no time.
You pinned me against the old stone—
kissing me with a hunger
that didn't care if the world saw.
Your hands slid up my dress,
fingers slipping past lace,
finding me soaked and silent—
my gasp caught in your mouth.
"You want to stop?"
"No," I breathed.
"Then keep quiet."
You knelt in the grass.
Lifted my leg to your shoulder.
And kissed me between my thighs
like it was *yours.*

I only heard the wet sounds
of your tongue and my moans
swallowed in your name.
I came shaking, back arched off the wall,
legs trembling as you stood,
kissed me hard—
and pressed yourself inside me
without a word.
It was wrong. It was risky. It was *us.*
And I'd risk it all again.

17. Pressed Into the Dunes

You kissed me like you were starving—
like your mouth had waited lifetimes
to ruin mine.
Deep, slow, possessive—
tongue tangling, lips grazing,
a moan caught between us
as you pressed me into the dunes.
Then your eyes dropped to my chest.
You didn't pull the bikini down.
You slid your hands beneath it—
palms warm, greedy—
cupping me like you'd claimed it all.
Your thumbs brushed my nipples,
light at first, teasing circles
until they hardened beneath your touch.
I gasped when you pinched,
bit my lip when you rolled them—
slow, skilled, *cruel.*
Then your mouth was on me,
sucking *through* the bikini,

tongue flicking, breath hot and wet,
until I arched up, whimpering,
begging you to take more.
And you did.
You pulled one cup aside,
wrapped your mouth around my nipple,
and sucked deep—
tongue swirling, lips sealed tight,
like you meant to finish me
before you ever touched below.
By the time your fingers slid lower,
I was already soaked, shaking,
and ready to let the sun watch me come.

18. Balcony Heat, Hotel Sin

We left the door open on purpose.
Ninth floor. City view.
Balcony too visible.
But I didn't care.
You unzipped my dress
and pushed me into the railing—
my chest bare to the night,
cool air kissing skin
your mouth was already claiming.
my breasts, squeezed, sucked,
bit down hard enough to make me gasp.
You feasted—mouth full of me,
tongue circling, teeth dragging—
until my moan echoed off the skyline.
Then you slipped inside from behind—
slow. thick. perfect.
"Someone could see," I whispered.
"I hope they do," you growled,
gripping my hip,
thrusting like the city below

didn't deserve the show.
I came holding the railing,
my cry swallowed by traffic.
You didn't stop.
You held me tight,
fucked me deeper—
until your groan cracked open the sky.
After, we stayed pressed together—
still joined, still breathless—
watching the world rush below
while we stood still
in our private, perfect crime.

19. We Never Sleep, We Just Sin

We didn't come here to rest.
We came to fuck
until the bed forgot how to hold us.
Sheets tangled, ice melted,
room service untouched–
your mouth full of me,
my nails dragging red down your back
as we ruined the room
and then did it again.
You licked honey off my nipple
and came between my thighs
with my name bitten into your lip.
Every hour, we started over.
You on your knees,
me riding you like worship,
both of us shaking with joy
that never once felt tiring.
I lost track of how many times I came.
You didn't.

You counted—whispering numbers in my ear,
like prayer, like proof.
We never closed our eyes.
We didn't need to.
Our bodies knew where to go—
always back to each other.
We didn't rest.
We *became* rest.
And still, I begged for more.

20. My Hell, Your Hands (The Vow)

You didn't rescue me.
You *wrecked me perfectly.*
With lips that never lied,
hands that never hesitated.

You fucked your promises
into my bones—
until I bent,
then begged for more.
You never said "forever."

You just stayed.
Again.
And again.

Now, when I tremble,
it's not from fear.
It's from remembering
how you made devotion

feel like being split open
and filled with something eternal.

21. Happy Fucking Ever After

We don't pretend anymore.
You want me—
messy, moaning, marked.
And I want you—
slow, deep, endless.
Every morning, your fingers find me
before the sun does.
Every night, we fall asleep
still tangled—
your hand between my thighs,
my mouth on your name.
We laugh now.
We fuck until we cry.
We fight.
We heal.
And when you whisper "mine,"
it's not possessive—
it's *home.*
This isn't perfect.

It’s ours.

Filthy. Feral. Forever.

Your hands.

My hell.

Our heaven.